THE INTERNAL COMBUSTION ENGINE

THE INTERNAL COMBUSTION ENGINE

ROSS R. OLNEY

illustrated by

STEVEN LINDBLOM

J. B. Lippincott   New York

Library of Congress Cataloging in Publication Data
Olney, Ross Robert, 1929–
The internal combustion engine.
Summary: Text and line drawings examine the parts of an engine
and how they work.
1. Internal combustion engines—Juvenile literature. [1. Internal
combustion engines. 2. Engines] I. Lindblom, Steven, ill. II. Title.
TJ755.5.045 1982   621.43′4   81-48604
ISBN 0-397-32009-4   AACR2
ISBN 0-397-32010-8 (lib. bdg.)

2   3   4   5   6   7   8   9   10
First Edition

THE INTERNAL COMBUSTION ENGINE

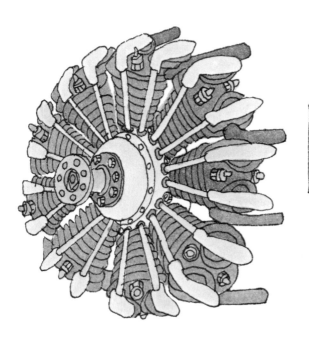

A Radial
Aircraft Engine
9 cylinders
220 h.p.

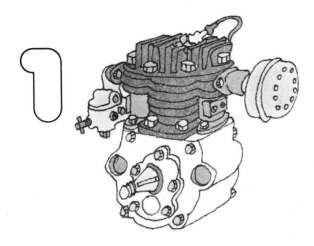

INTERNAL COMBUSTION ENGINES are engines that burn their fuel *inside.* The engine in your family car is probably an internal combustion engine. Most likely, it burns gasoline or diesel fuel inside its cylinders to create power to move the car.

Internal combustion engines do more than move cars. If every internal combustion engine in the world suddenly stopped, your own town would grind to a halt. Cars would stop, yes. Most buses would stop, too. The lights might go out since electricity is often generated by internal combustion engines. The hospital would probably have to close its doors. The radio and TV stations would go off the air.

But this won't happen. Internal combustion engines work very well. Better than any other type of engine. They are one of the best sources of power we have.

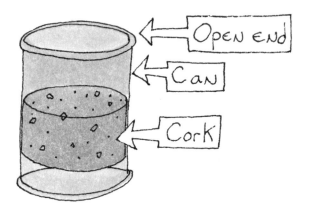

A CORK AND A CAN

Imagine a large, clean, shiny tin can. The can has been opened. It is empty. This can is just like the *cylinder* in an internal combustion engine.

Now imagine a large cork that just fits into the can. The cork is like the *piston* in an engine.

Go ahead, plug the cork into the can in your imagination. Shove it all the way in. All you can see is the bottom of the cork down inside the can.

Now turn the can upside down. The closed end of the can is up. The cork is inside the can.

Here's where the experiment gets tricky. The job is to move the cork toward the open end of the can. This is what a piston does in a cylinder of an engine.

MOVING THE CORK

The truth is, people have known how to move the cork (piston) in the can (cylinder) for ages. The ancient Romans knew how to do it. So did the ancient Greeks. You might know how to do it, too.

How about this? Punch a little hole in the closed end of the can and *blow* in. This turns the can into an oversized beanshooter. The compressed air could

move the cork if it isn't stuck into the can too tight.

Forcing some steam into the closed end of the can could also move the cork. Steam is easy to make, by boiling water, and it creates a pressure. The cork would begin to move out of the can.

Too much steam and the cork would pop out of the can with great force.

If the tin can was very strong and very smooth inside, it would be like a cylinder in a steam engine. If the cork was metal and fit perfectly inside the cylinder, it would be like a piston for a steam engine. When the steam pressed into the cylinder, the piston would move.

The moving piston could do work. How that happens will be covered later in this book. Here, all we want to do is get the piston moving in the cylinder.

Using steam to do it, we'd have an *external* com-

bustion engine. Or at least one cylinder from such an engine.

Why *external?* Because the steam has to be made somewhere outside the cylinder and then piped in. It is usually made in a nearby boiler. Then it gets to the cylinder through a pipe. Steam engines are still used today for many jobs.

INTERNAL COMBUSTION

It would be even better if the piston could be moved without steam. Then the engine wouldn't need a big part like a boiler to make the steam.

What if the piston could be moved with a pressure made *inside* the cylinder? There are some ways. It would be foolish and unsafe, but the piston could be moved with some dynamite inside the cylinder. When the dynamite exploded, the piston would move.

That is, if the whole cylinder didn't just blow apart! The pressure made by the explosion of dynamite must go somewhere. It is trapped inside the cylinder. So it moves the piston trying to get out. With too large an explosion, the piston would probably fly out of the cylinder just like a bullet from a gun.

Before we have pistons flying all over the place, remember this. The idea is to move the piston in the cylinder in a *controlled* way. The idea is to do it with a pressure created inside the cylinder.

There were people thinking about this a long time ago. One was an inventor who had a new idea. His name was the Reverend W. Cecil.

THE REVEREND CECIL'S SPEECH

There was a meeting of scientists and inventors in Cambridge, England, in 1820. Everybody took turns talking about their ideas and inventions. But the others laughed when the Reverend Cecil began to speak. Back then, people thought that everything important had already been invented. Especially everything about engines. Engines were as perfect as people could make them. What could be better than a steam engine, after all?

Even though these were scientists who were supposed to believe in new ideas, not many of them believed the Reverend Cecil. But then this was the first time that anybody had ever tried to explain *internal* combustion, so maybe they can be forgiven.

Cecil was sure he knew how to make a piston move in a cylinder *without* steam from outside. He was trying to get them to believe he could move the piston by burning a gas *inside the cylinder.* The burning gas would quickly expand and force the piston to move.

How foolish, they shouted from the audience. There were far too many problems for this to ever work. Nobody would believe such wild ideas. Many of them thought the Reverend Cecil was telling a joke. So most of them just laughed and enjoyed it.

Often people will laugh at somebody with a new idea. But Cecil had worked this idea out with a model. He knew his new internal combustion engine would work.

THE REVEREND CECIL was right, though his model has long since been lost. He was the first to explain internal combustion. Now everybody knows that fuel can be burned inside a cylinder to make a piston move. It isn't even very difficult once the basic idea is understood. The burning fuel creates a great pressure.

Look under the hood of your own family car. What a maze of metal parts and wires and tubes! But each part has a job. By the time you have finished this book, you will recognize most of the parts of this very important machine.

According to scientists (*not* those from the Reverend Cecil's day) there is a reason why internal combustion engines are so good. The reason is, they are very light in weight for the amount of power they produce. They don't weigh very much for the amount of work they can do. Yes, an engine can be very heavy. But compared to other types of engines, the internal combustion engine is not heavy.

THE INTERNAL COMBUSTION ENGINE

A *piston* is moved in a *cylinder*.

The Reverend Cecil knew it could be moved by a force from within. But whether it is moved from outside with steam or from inside with burning fuel, what's the difference? A piston just moving in a cylinder can't really do much of *anything*.

That is, it couldn't until French inventor Jean Joseph E'tienne Lenoir came along. Lenoir thought of a way to make Cecil's idea work. He invented the first *practical* internal combustion engine in 1860. In fact, in 1863 Lenoir built one of the very first gas-engine cars in the world.

In those days, gas was used to light street lamps. Lenoir needed a fuel that would burn, so he used streetlight gas. He ignited the gas inside the cylinder. The burning gas created a pressure that moved the piston.

THE CRANKSHAFT

Lenoir borrowed an idea from steam engines to use in his engine. He attached the piston to a *crankshaft*. The crankshaft is the key to the operation of every engine, internal or external. It takes the straight-line motion of the piston in the cylinder and turns it into a circular motion. Then if one spinning end of the crankshaft is sticking out of the engine, work can be done.

Lenoir knew that the spinning shaft could make the wheels of a car move. Or it could have a pulley on it to drive a generator for electric power. A spinning shaft could have a gear on it to do many other kinds of work.

Consider a one-cylinder engine. At first, only one-cylinder engines were built. Lenoir's engines were one-cylinder types. They were used in Paris, France, to power printing presses, lathes, and water pumps, and then his car.

A one-cylinder engine has a crankshaft with one offset section that works almost like the pedal on a bike. See the illustration on page 12. There is a connection between the piston and the offset section of the crankshaft (called the *journal*). When the piston moves up and down, the crankshaft spins around.

Watch your own knee and foot when you pedal
your bike. Don't stare at it so much that you don't look
ahead, of course. You'll see that as your knee goes up
and down (the piston) your foot goes around and
around (the crankshaft journal). The axle of the
bike-chain sprocket is turning around due to the up-
and-down motion of your knee. The pedals are the
offset journals of the crankshaft.

THE CONNECTING ROD
Your leg from your knee to your foot is the "engine's"
connecting rod. That is exactly what it is called in a

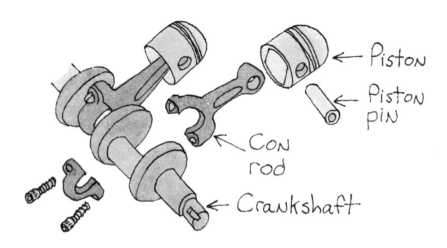

← Piston

← Piston pin

← Con rod

← Crankshaft

real engine. It is attached to the crankshaft at one end and to the piston (with a *piston pin*) at the other end.

You've heard of "throwing a rod" in an engine. Race cars sometimes do this because they are forced to go very fast and work very hard. So do some passenger cars. This means that the rod between the piston and the crankshaft has broken. Or at least one of the rods since most modern car engines have several.

More about these bigger engines later.

ENGINE BUILDERS DO NOT use corks and tin
cans. They use parts that are very carefully made of
strong metal. The parts all fit together just right. The
piston fits into the cylinder very well.

PISTON RINGS

To be sure of a good fit, *piston rings* are added
around the top of the piston. These rings fit into slots
around the piston. Nothing can squeeze past the
rings if everything fits just right. Not even the pressure from the gases of burning fuel. So the piston is
moved and the crankshaft turns.

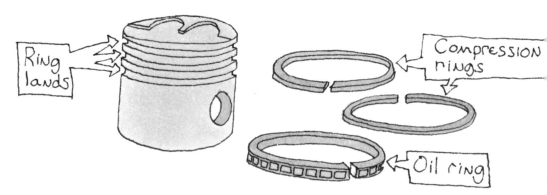

If the rings wear out, then the engine won't work as well as it did. Sometimes an engine needs a "ring job." This means the engine needs new piston rings. The expanding gases from the burning fuel are squeezing past the old rings because they are worn. Power is being lost.

Another job of the piston rings is to carry oil up the inside walls of the cylinder. This helps the parts slide against each other without wearing out. More about this in the section on lubrication.

VALVES

The real problem was how to get fuel into each cylinder. And how to get the exhaust gases out. Steam was easy. You just punched a hole and kept squirting in steam when you wanted the piston to move. The piston would come back to the closed end of the cylinder because of the force of the spinning crankshaft. Then more steam would be squirted in. This would keep the piston moving.

Inventors tried many ways to get fuel inside the cylinder. Some of the inventions blew up. Others just didn't work right.

Finally, *valves* that would work with fuel were designed. Nobody knows who thought of them first. They work best of all.

Remember the tin can? What if we just cut two big holes in the closed end of the can? One hole could be

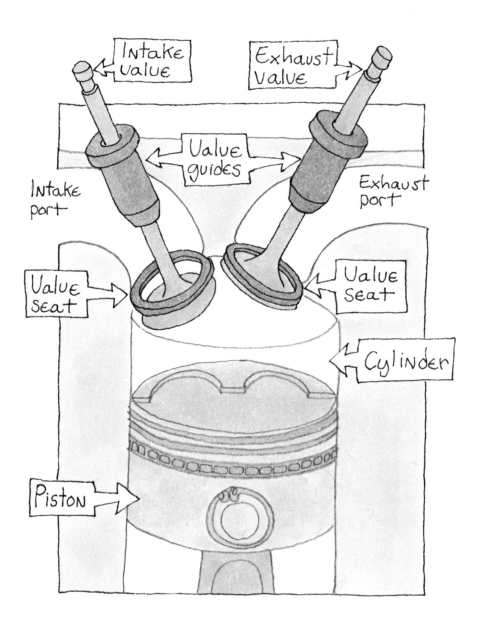

Intake
Value

Exhaust
Value

Value
guides

Intake
port

Exhaust
port

Value
Seat

Value
Seat

Cylinder

Piston

to get fuel in. The other could be to allow burned gases to get out. The first hole could be called the "intake" hole and the second the "exhaust."

But wait a minute! If we cut two holes in the top of the cylinder (called the *cylinder head*), won't the pressure leak out? And if the pressure leaks out, the piston won't move.

Yes, so builders put plugs in each hole. Plugs that move. These plugs are the valves. They fit very tightly so that no pressure can leak out. If pressure does leak out, the engine probably needs a "valve job." This means that the valves need grinding and polishing so they fit just right again. More about how valves open and close in just a minute.

BUT WHAT ABOUT A BIG ENGINE?

What about an engine with more than one cylinder? And more than one piston, since each cylinder has a piston? And valves in each cylinder? After all, a one-cylinder engine isn't very powerful. You can hold some of them in your hand, like a model-airplane engine or a lawn-mower engine.

You can probably think of others. But you can't run a bus with a little one-cylinder engine. Most cars have four- six-, or eight-cylinder engines. Some have twelve or even sixteen cylinders. No matter how many cylinders there are, each cylinder has its own piston and its own valves. Each piston, though, is

connected to a *single* crankshaft by a connecting rod. In this way, each piston is helping to turn one main crankshaft. A lot of power is going to that one crankshaft.

Picture it this way. Imagine a bicycle-built-for-two. Or four. Or *eight!*

But instead of being in a long row, the riders are pedaling side by side. There is one main axle running through all the pedal sprockets.

This would be pretty funny. The contraption would fill the street from curb to curb.

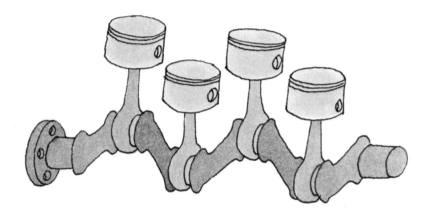

But it is an easy way to see what the crankshaft is doing in an engine with more than one cylinder. On the bike, each knee is a piston and each lower leg is a connecting rod. They all push up and down, and turn, to spin the one main shaft. That's how an engine with several cylinders works. Power is taken off the end of the crankshaft to do work, just as a strong chain might be driving one rear wheel of the foolish-looking bicycle.

Of course, in an engine everything is smaller and the parts work better together.

THE FOUR-STROKE-CYCLE INTERNAL COMBUSTION ENGINE

In most car engines, each piston moves up and down *twice* for each "power stroke." Some smaller engines don't work this way, but we'll think about car engines here.

The piston is shoved by expanding gases and turns the crankshaft. Then the exhaust valve pops open. As the piston moves back to the closed end of the cylinder, it shoves the burned gases out through the exhaust valve hole. Then the exhaust valve closes.

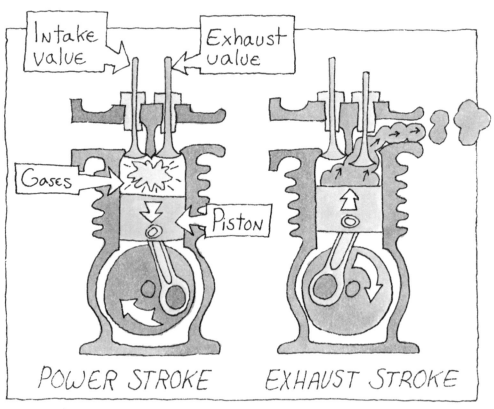

Intake Valve

Exhaust Valve

Gases

Piston

POWER STROKE   EXHAUST STROKE

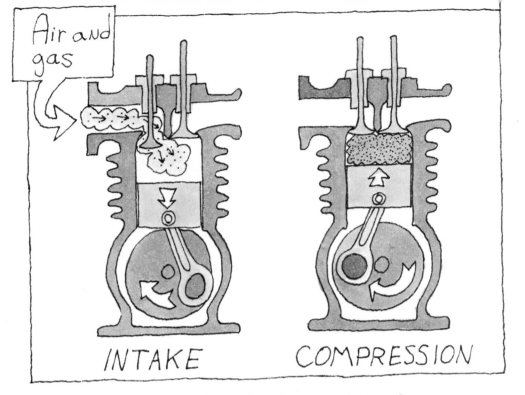

Air and gas

INTAKE　　　**COMPRESSION**

The piston moves down for the second time because the crankshaft is turning. The intake valve pops open. A new fuel-air mixture rushes in through the intake valve. Then the intake valve closes. The fuel mixture is trapped inside.

The piston starts back up to the closed end of the cylinder again. This time *no* valves are open. The cylinder is sealed tight. So the piston squeezes the air and fuel mixture very tightly. It has nowhere to go. In fact, the measure of "compression" of an engine is how tightly the fuel mixture is squeezed by the piston. Some engines squeeze it tighter in a smaller space than others.

IGNITION!

At just the right instant, the fuel is ignited. It burns, expands the air quickly, and forces the piston to move back down again. The piston turns the crankshaft. Then it starts back up, forcing out the exhaust gases since the exhaust valve has opened. This happens over and over for each cylinder of the engine. It happens hundreds of times every minute if the engine is running fast.

The valves must open and close at just the right time. And they must fit perfectly.

The next chapter will explain what opens and closes them with such exact timing.

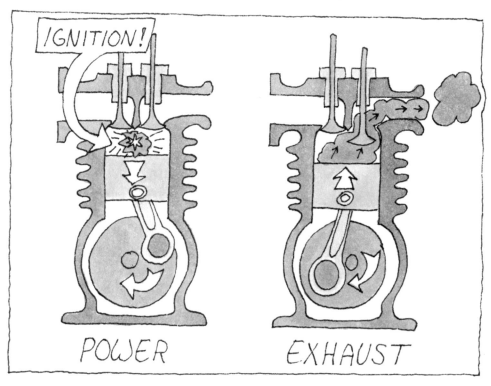

POWER   EXHAUST

MANY THINGS MUST WORK just right for an internal combustion engine to operate.

THE FUEL

Fuel must enter the cylinder ready to burn. Before it gets to the intake valve, it must be made ready.

On some gasoline-powered engines and all diesel engines, the fuel is squirted directly into the cylinders. This is called "fuel injection."

But on most standard engines, a *carburetor* mixes raw gasoline with air. Just the right amount of gaso-

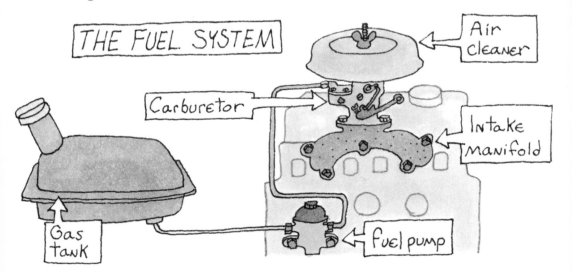

THE FUEL SYSTEM

Air cleaner

Carburetor

Intake Manifold

Gas tank

Fuel pump

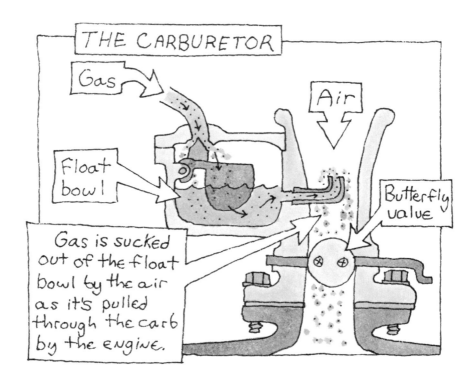

THE CARBURETOR

Gas

Air

Float bowl

Butterfly valve

Gas is sucked out of the float bowl by the air as it's pulled through the carb by the engine.

line to just the right amount of air. This makes a mist of gasoline and air. The gasoline, meanwhile, is being pumped to the carburetor by a *fuel pump.*

Take another look at the engine in your family car. On top there will be a big, round can. In the can is an air filter. The air that goes into an engine must be very clean. So it goes through the filter and then into the carburetor. The carburetor is just under the filter.

The misty fuel mixture from the carburetor goes into an "intake manifold." Then the intake valve pops open on a cylinder and the fuel mixture rushes in to be burned.

The row of valves on the tops of the cylinders jerk open and shut in a blur when the engine is running. They are controlled by a *camshaft.* This is a funny-looking thing that seems more like a junk part. All along the camshaft are egg-shaped sections. There are as many of these *lobes* as there are valves in the engine.

Imagine rolling an egg across a table, end over end. It will go up and down, up and down, as the long end and then the short end rolls over.

Now imagine the egg spinning on an axle that has been shoved through it. Put your finger against the egg as it spins. Your finger is pushed up and down. This is how the valves in an engine are pushed open and then allowed to close. In fact, the lobes on a camshaft look very much like a row of eggs.

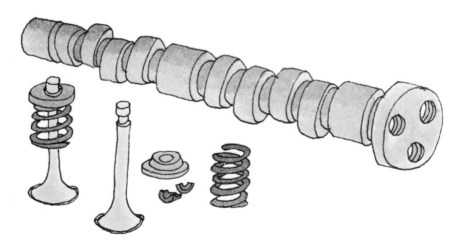

The high point on the lobes pushes the valves open. Then a very strong *valve spring* snaps them shut. But in the meantime, fuel has entered or exhaust gases have escaped.

On an "overhead cam" engine, the camshaft is at the top. The lobes press directly on the valves. On a "pushrod" engine, the lobes push on rods. The rods push on *rocker arms,* and the rocker arms push on the valves. In this type of engine, the camshaft is down inside the engine.

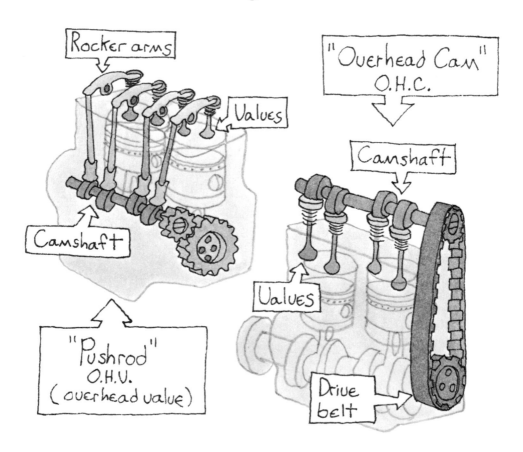

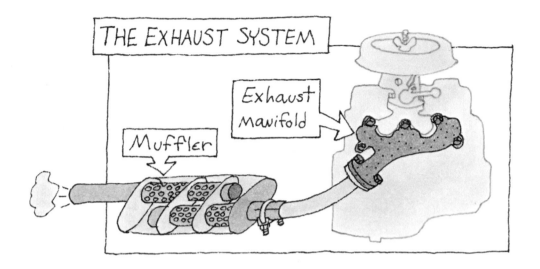

EXHAUST

Burned gases are pushed out through the exhaust valve and into the *exhaust manifold.* This is just a collecting area for the gases from all the cylinders in the engine.

Pressure from new gases coming in keeps everything moving along. The gases flow into one or more exhaust pipes attached to the exhaust manifold.

Then they go to the *muffler.* This looks like a big tin can under the car. It helps to cut down on the noise of the fuel burning in the cylinders. Race cars usually do not have a muffler, and they are very loud. Drag racers don't even have long exhaust pipes. They are so loud the noise can injure your ears. Burning fuel inside an engine makes a lot of noise.

Many metal parts are moving about inside an internal combustion engine. Connecting rods are moving up and down and around. The crankshaft is spinning. The camshaft is spinning. Most of these parts are moving in *bearings.*

Bearings are used between metal parts that must move or spin together. The bearings keep the metal parts from rubbing together.

Squeeze your hand around a baseball bat or some other round pipe. Try to spin the bat or pipe. The bat will be impossible to spin if you are holding it tightly.

Now put a piece of wax paper between your hand and the bat. See how much easier the bat spins even if you are holding tightly? The wax paper is like a bearing.

An engine crankshaft is held by large bearings. The camshaft is held by smaller bearings because it is smaller. There are bearings between the connecting rods and the offset journals on the crankshaft.

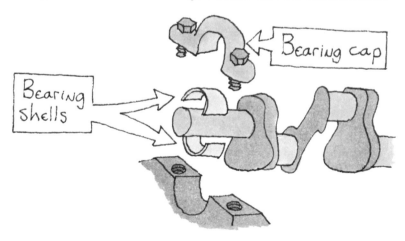

Bearing cap

Bearing shells

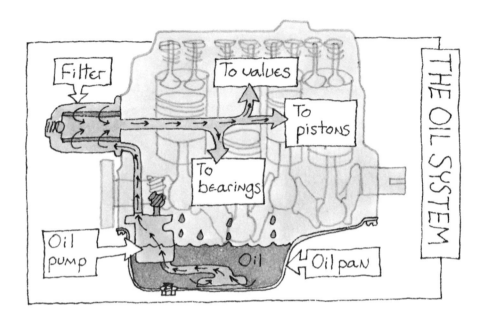

LUBRICATION

Every part in an engine needs lubrication or the engine will overheat. It could grind itself to pieces. Sometimes, if lubrication fails in an internal combustion engine, parts melt from the heat.

So oil is added. Most internal combustion engines have an *oil pump* at the bottom. This is where the oil goes when you add it. It waits there for the oil pump to pick it up. The oil pump forces oil to every moving part of the engine. There must be a thin film of oil on the bearings and on metal parts that slide against each other.

If you would soak the wax paper in oil before grabbing the baseball bat, the bat would spin even easier.

Piston rings help to bring oil to the cylinder walls. Oil is squirted into the crankshaft and camshaft bearings. It is squirted into the bearing between the connecting rod and the crankshaft. It is squirted into the connection between the connecting rod and the piston pin. The spinning crankshaft splashes oil around inside the engine.

The oil is pumped through an *oil filter* to help keep it clean. Dirty oil is hard on an internal combustion engine.

Eventually, the oil drips back into the pan at the bottom of the engine. There it is picked up again by the pump and started on another trip through the engine. There is always extra oil in the pan. An engine would soon stop if the oil supply ran out.

This could happen if there was an oil leak somewhere. Or if the engine burned away all its oil. If the piston rings go bad, oil can leak up into the closed end of the cylinder. Then it is burned away with the fuel mixture.

If you see a smoky engine, it is probably burning some of its oil along with the fuel.

OIL HELPS TO KEEP the engine cool. But that isn't the only cooling an engine gets. Except for certain air-cooled engines, the *radiator* is the main cooling unit on an internal combustion engine.

Engines that use a radiator for cooling have two walls. All of the hot parts are double-thick, with a space in between. Water with some antifreeze (to keep the water from freezing in the winter when the engine is off) is put in. The water doesn't get too hot because it is piped to the radiator through *radiator hoses.* A *water pump* keeps it moving from the engine to the radiator and back.

A fan at the front of most engines keeps air moving through the radiator. This helps to carry away the heat from the water coming from the engine.

If one of the hoses or connections develops a leak, the water can drip out. Sometimes this happens. As the water leaks out, the engine gets hotter and hotter. An internal combustion engine must be kept at the right temperature. If it gets too hot, it won't run right. It can even get so hot that it simply "locks up." Too

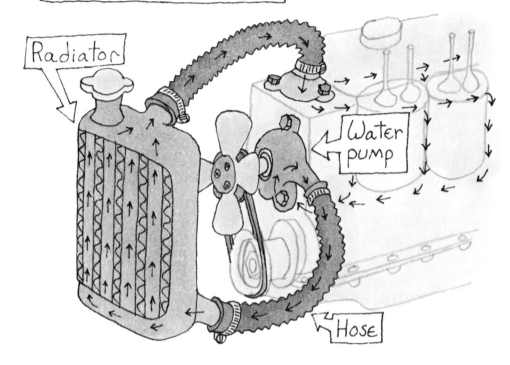

COOLING SYSTEM

Radiator

Water pump

Hose

much heat is very bad for an internal combustion engine.

But it is also bad for an engine to run too *cool*. The engine must be operated at a nice warm temperature, not too hot and not too cold. Most engines have a gauge to indicate the correct operating temperature. And a *thermostat* to control the temperature of the water.

Air-cooled internal combustion engines do not have water flowing around them. They are cooled by a flow of air over their cylinders. Many of them have "fins" to help keep them cool. The fins give the heat more metal to get to before the cooling air carries it away. The best known air-cooled internal combustion engine is the Volkswagen engine.

But your lawn mower probably has an air-cooled internal combustion engine, too.

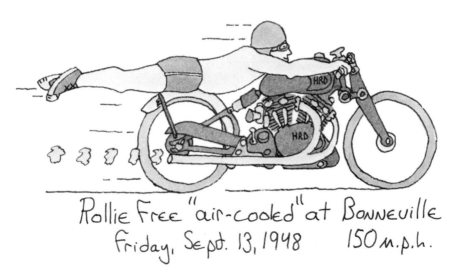

Rollie Free "air-cooled" at Bonneville
Friday, Sept. 13, 1948   150 m.p.h.

THE PISTONS ARE MOVING up and down in their cylinders. The fuel is burning and expanding to make them move.

The pistons are spinning the crankshaft to produce power for whatever the engine is built to do.

The valves are opening and closing at the right time.

Fuel is flowing in and exhaust gases are flowing out.

The camshaft is spinning to move the valves.

The oil is lubricating the engine.

The radiator water and antifreeze are cooling the engine.

The fuel pump is pumping fuel to the carburetor. The water pump is pumping water. The oil pump is pumping oil.

You know about the connecting rods and bearings. What else is there?

Wait a minute! What makes the whole thing work? An internal combustion engine must *combust internally.* There must be some way to *ignite* the fuel to make it burn.

THE IGNITION SYSTEM

This is where the *spark plugs* come in. If the spark plugs aren't working, nothing will work.

A misty mixture of gasoline and air is a very dangerous vapor. Scientists say it is more powerful than TNT.

If you squeeze such a mixture into a metal cylinder by pushing on it with a tightly fitting piston, you have power ready to happen!

A spark could set it off in an instant.

That is just what happens. The spark plug sparks

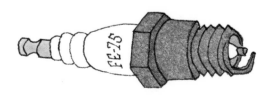

inside the cylinder and the fuel mixture ignites. The spark is just like any other spark you have seen. It jumps between two *electrodes* at the bottom of the spark plug. These are just two little metal prongs. They stick down into the cylinder.

The spark must jump at just the right instant. That is the job of the *ignition system.*

IGNITION SYSTEM PARTS

The heart of the system on most internal combustion engines is a battery. Your family car has a battery. The battery produces the voltage to get the engine going. And to keep it going. Voltage is electric power.

If you have a "dead" battery, you have a battery with no voltage. Your engine will not start.

The battery does other things, too. It lights the lights of the car and it works the radio. It does many electrical jobs. But it doesn't seem to run out of "juice" very often. Most engines have something to keep the battery full of electric voltage. This is called an *alternator* on cars. As long as the engine is running, the alternator is making voltage to keep the battery charged and the spark plugs sparking.

Here's how it all works together.

Voltage coming from the battery is sent to the *distributor.* The amount of voltage is controlled by a *voltage regulator.*

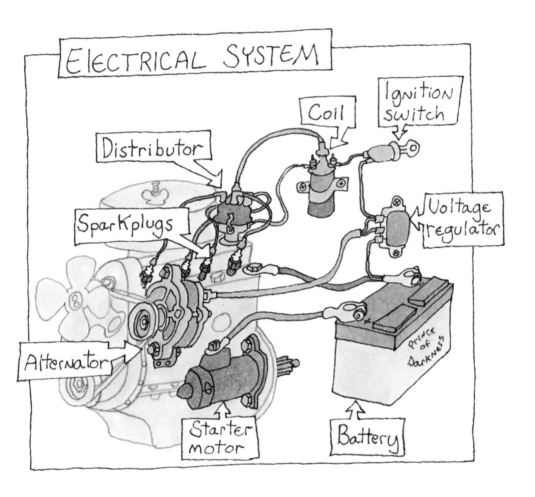

ELECTRICAL SYSTEM

Coil

Ignition switch

Distributor

Voltage regulator

Spark plugs

Alternator

Starter motor

Battery

prince of darkness

The distributor has heavy wires going to the spark plugs. If there are four spark plugs, there will be four wires. It is the job of the distributor to tell which plug to spark at which time.

It takes a large amount of voltage to make the spark jump inside the cylinder. There isn't enough voltage in the battery. Not even if the alternator is working very hard. So a *coil* is used. This is a part that builds up voltage. A small amount of voltage goes into a coil, and a much larger amount comes out. The distributor then sends this larger voltage to the spark plugs, one by one.

Fuel mixture ignites and burns and one piston is moved, then the next, then the next. So the crankshaft keeps spinning. When one piston is moving up to push out the exhaust gases, another is moving down with a power stroke. A third might be somewhere in between. It might be compressing a new fuel mixture for the next power stroke. The fourth piston in the engine might be drawing in new fuel. On engines with a number of pistons, two might be doing the same job. The distributor knows where each piston is and when to send the spark.

None of this matters on a one-cylinder engine. The one piston is going up or down. There aren't any more. But a one-cylinder engine has a distributor, too —a very simple one.

As you have probably guessed, the distributor is turned by the engine itself. It is geared to the good old crankshaft. When the crankshaft spins, everything seems to go to work.

DIESEL

A fuel injection system takes the place of both carburetor and distributor, shooting the fuel in at just the right moment!

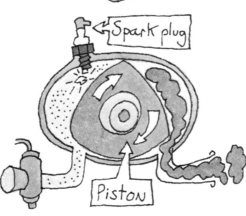

ROTARY

The rotary has a three-sided "piston" which rotates in the cylinder. Three of the four strokes can be going on at the same time!

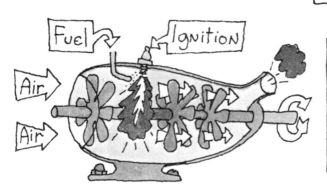

TURBINE

Burning fuel spins propeller-like blades, which turn the drive-shaft.

There are different types of internal combustion engines. All work because of fuel burning *inside* them. A *diesel* engine works with pistons in cylinders, but without spark plugs. They aren't needed in a diesel. The fuel is squeezed so hard by the pistons in a diesel that it heats up and catches fire all by itself.

A *rotary* engine has a different type of piston. But it is still expanding gases that moves this round "piston."

Even a *turbine* engine is an internal combustion engine. It works in a different way. It has spinning propeller blades inside instead of pistons. So does a *jet* engine, still another type of internal combustion engine.

But they all burn their fuel inside, just like the one we know best . . . the automobile engine.